Listen, here's the thing.

If you can't spot the sucker
in your first half hour at the table,

then you are the sucker.

Guys around here'll tell ya...
you play for a living.

It's like any other job.
You don't gamble. You grind it out.

Your goal is to win
one big bet an hour, that's it.

Get your money in when you have the best
of it, and protect it when you don't.

Don't give anything away.

That's how I've paid my way
through half of law school.

A true grinder.

See, I learned how to win a little at
a time. But finally, I've learned this...

If you're too careful, your
whole life can become a fuckin' grind.

This is Teddy KGB's place.

- Five hundred.
- You won't find it in the Yellow Pages.

Nope.
Not tonight.

No? What?

Give me three stacks of high society.

Thirty thousand.
Count it.

- That's good.
- So, you're sitting the apple.

- Good. Want a cookie?
- No.

He doesn't look like much,

but KGB is connected all the way
to the top of the Russian mob.

He's the one guy in the game
you don't want to fuck with.

But if you're looking for high stakes,

this is the only place in town.

They all know me as a small-timer,
but that's about to change.

Joey Knish is a New York legend.

He's been a rounder,
earning his living at cards...

since he was 19 years old.

What are you, holdin' those for somebody?

Uh, yeah, I'm holding 'em for you.

You should be.

'Cause I hope you're not thinking
of putting all that glimmer in play.

He's as close to a friend
as there is in this place.

- Come here.
- But tonight, I don't want to see him.

Now, you don't wanna
butt onions with these guys.

'Cause they'll chew you up,
take your whole bankroll.

- So you say.
- There's plenty of easy games.

We get outta here, get some coffee,
ride over to that soft seat in Queens.

I know what I'm doing.

You're making a run at it, aren't you?

Rolling up a stake and going to Vegas.

I'm right, right?

- I can beat the game.
- Maybe.

Maybe this is a game can be beat.

But you know you can beat the 10-20
at the Chesterfield and the Hi-Low...

at that goulash joint on 79th Street.

Okay.
I understand.

I understand.
Back to battle.

The game in question is
No-Limit Texas Hold 'Em.

Minimum buy-in $25,000.

A game like this doesn't come together
often outside the casinos.

The stakes attract rich flounders,

and they in turn attract the sharks.

No-Limit Texas Hold 'Em
is the Cadillac of poker.

Each player is dealt two cards face down.

Five cards are then dealt
face up across the middle.

These are community cards everyone can
use to make the best five card hand.

The key to the game is playing
the man, not the cards.

Bet an eight ball.

There's no other game in which fortunes
can change so much from hand to hand.

A brilliant player can get

a strong hand cracked, go on tilt...

and lose his mind along with
every single chip in front of him.

This is why the World Series of Poker is
decided over a No-Limit Hold 'Em table.

Some people, pros even,
won't play No-Limit.

They can't handle the swings.

But there are others, like Doyle Brunson,

who consider No-Limit
the only pure game left.

Like Papa Wallenda said..."Life is on
the wire. The rest is just waiting."

Pass it to you.

All right, I raise.

- I'm gonna raise five hundred.
- Fold.

It's a position raise.
I call it.

Here's the beauty of this game.

- Go ahead.
- I just got top two pair on the flop,

and I want to keep him in the hand.

Against your average guy,
I'd set a bear trap, hardly bet at all.

Let him walk into it.
But KGB's too smart for that.

So, what I've got to do
is over-bet the pot,

make it look like I'm trying to buy it.

- I bet $2,000.
- Then he plays back at me,
and I get paid off.

Call.

My guess is Teddy's on a flush draw.

Burn and turn.

There's my money card, nine of hearts.

I got a full house.

- To the bettor.
- Check's good.

Now I hope
a spade falls and Teddy makes his flush.

That way he'll bet strong, and I'll beat
him with my nines full over aces.

I'm going to bet...

Bet...

$15,000.

Time.

I want him to think that I'm pondering a call,

but all I'm really thinking about
is Vegas and the fucking Mirage.

All right, your 15, plus
I have another 33 to raise you.

Um...

Yeah, I'm gonna go all in, 'cause
I don't think you got the spades.

You are right.
I don't have spades.

I know before the cards are even turned over.

Aces full, Mike.

Get up.

Come on.
Come on.

- Want some?
- No.

I'm down to the felt, Knish.
I lost everything.

Man, I lost my case money.
I lost my tuition.

It happens to everyone.
Time to time, everyone goes bust.

You'll be back in the game before you know it.

I'm done.

I'm out of it.

They all say that at first.

Hey, man, let me stake you.
Standard deal, you know.

Fifty percent of your winnings.
If you lose, it's on me.

I'd just throw it away.

- You still got the truck?
- Sure.

Come on.

You don't hear much
about guys who take their shot and miss,

but I'll tell you what happens to 'em.

They end up humping crappy jobs
on graveyard shifts,

trying to figure out how they came up short.

See, I had this picture in my head.

Me sitting at the big table, Doyle to my left,

Amarillo Slim to my right,
playing in the World Series of Poker.

And I let that vision
blind me at the table against KGB.

Now, the closest I get
to Vegas is west New York,

driving this lousy route
handed down from Knish...

to rounders who forget
the cardinal fuckin' rule...

Always leave yourself outs.

- Hey, Moogie.
- Let me ask you a question.

In a legal sense, can fuckin'
Steinbrenner just move the Yankees?

Does he have the fuckin' right
to just move them?

I don't know.
How should I know that?

- You didn't learn that yet?
- No, we get to Steinbrenner
in the third year of law school.

Oh.

- Take care, man.
- Yeah.

The judges' game.

I'd heard about it for years on the
street, before I was even in law school.

A rotating group of ten or twelve
judges, prosecutors and professors.

They all have money, and in my playing days...

it would have been pretty sweet to have

any one of them owing me favors.

Only problem is, no one
can get in the game anymore.

One rounder, Crispy Linetta,
sat under some pretense,

but they found out he was a pro,
he couldn't cross the street
without a legal hassle.

Even his regular club, Vorshay's, got shut down.

Place had been open since 1907.

Oh, Michael.

- You got some things for me?
- Yes, I do.

Put 'em on the desk, it's all right.

Kid, he paying you for this late night shit?

Oh, well, knowledge is my reward, sir.

Let me tell you, it ain't worth it.

Why don't you become a jockey,
do something useful.

Kid's a little tall, isn't he, Gene?

Enough with the Belmont
recruiting spiel. Your bet.

- All right. I call.
- Michael is lead counsel...

in the Moot Court
you're presiding over next week, Gene.

Besides, he could use
the background if he's gonna...

clerk for one of you fellas this summer, right?

Abe, I thought you liked the kid. Why do
you want to make him a civil servant?

Yeah, look... a word to the wise.
Stay in the private sector.

That Nassau defense attorney's game?
They use our chips for coasters.

The amazing thing is, in this
collection of great legal minds,

there isn't a single real card player.

- I call.
- Raise.

Um, the professor raises.

Mike?
Michael, I would have just called.

No, you're good.

All right, I call.

I don't know if I'm going to bring
my legal career to a crashing halt...

before it even starts,
but I just can't help myself.

- Good.
- I'm in.

Read 'em and weep.

Threes check.

Check to Martin and Lewis over there.

- Check to the raiser.
- Czechoslovakia.

- What's the limit?
- $20. Big bet's $20.

Okay. Good.
There's $20.

You've seen half a hand. How the
fuck are you betting into us?

You sure this is wise, Abe?
It's your money the kid's bettin' with.

It's plenty wise.
We know what we're holding,
and we know what you're holding.

The fuck you know what we all got.

Summer clerkship in your office says
I know what you're holding.

I don't bet with jobs like that.

Let's just say I'll put you at the top
of the list if you're right.

Okay. Well, you were looking for that third three,

but you forgot that Professor Green
folded it on Fourth Street,

and now you're representing that you have it.

The D.A. made his two pair,
but he knows they're no good.

Judge Kaplan was trying to squeeze out
a diamond flush, but he came up short,

and Mr. Eisen is futilely hoping
that his queens are gonna stand up.

So, like I said, the Dean's bet is $20.

- Well, kiss my ass.
- Kiss my ass.

- What'd you have, Abe?
- Nothin' but a busted straight.

- Oh, come on.
- It's good enough to win. Take it down.

All right, kid, your first assignment.
Pull up a seat next to me.

Oh, I'd like to. I can't, I can't.
I don't play cards.

- Get outta here!
- See you tomorrow.

- Whose deal?
- My deal.

- I like the kid, Abe.
- Good kid.

Smart kid.

I tell ya, it's hard leaving that game.

An open invitation to lay with those lambs.

But I'm retired.

The truth is, I can always find games, though.

Easy games, tough games, straight games, crooked games, home games.

I can turn this truck onto the Jersey Turnpike and be at the Taj in two hours.

But I've made promises.

I'm just a law student now.

Hello?

- Hey.
- Hey.

- How'd it go?
- Oh, great.

I am sick of that fucking route.

Don't worry.
A few more semesters...

Mmm.

Oh, I gotta go.

- I'm really late.
- Oh, just stay here. I'll be really quick.

You won't feel a thing.

We both know that's not true.

Besides, you should get some sleep.

These fuckin' long nights are killing me.

They never used to.

Yeah, well, that's different.
I mean, that was like...

buy in at 8:00, next thing
you know it's morning.

But hey, you know, I think
I'm hooked up for this summer.

Hooked up how?

Well, after I left you last night at the
library, I impressed Judge Marinacci.

I think I might be in line for a clerkship.

Tell me more.

Well, those guys were all playing cards, and...

Just hear me out now, hear me out.

They were playing cards
and I read his hand blind.

So, instead of coming home, you went
and played cards with some judge?

No, I wasn't even playing.
They were playing.

I just caught his eye
by reading his hand, that's all.

I mean, as long as I don't fuck
up Moot Court, I think the job's mine.

What kind of job is that gonna be, Mike?

Writing an opinion
on high-stakes poker?

Honey, you're the one who told me...

that I should use my poker skills
in the courtroom.

Yeah, I know I said that, but...

You know what I meant.
I meant that you should use your head.

You know, the way you calculate odds
on the spot, the way you read people.

That's what I meant.
I didn't mean that you should try to
con your way into a summer job.

- Honey, con? I was networking.
- Oh, God.

Networking. Are you trying
to con me now?

No.

I just...
I don't think you get it.

You'll be just like one
of those ex-college athletes.

You know, great job at the
D.A. 's office as long as...

they never miss a lawyer's league game.

It's true. I just think if you
get in this way,

you'll always be a hustler to them.

Baby, I didn't even play.

Okay.

I'll see you later.

Oh.

- Hey, hon, can I take
the Jeep tomorrow?
- Yeah, where?

Uh, Worm's gettin' out.
I was gonna pick him up.

Tomorrow.
Beautiful.

I promised I'd be there, hon.

Worm. I just can't believe you
still know someone called "Worm."

He's like my brother.

Shit.
I didn't even play.

I met Worm
at Dwight Inglewood Preparatory
Academy over in Jersey.

We were the only two kids attending
who didn't have a trust fund.

My father's office was there.
It said "Custodian" on the door.

That's why they took me.

Pow!

W-Was that, like,
your strong finish or something?

- Motherfucker!
- You leave me no choice,
the way you play.

That's the fourth time you done
played that bitch of spades on my ass.

No, no, no, no, no.

Dowling had it three hands ago, and
two hands ago I got the black Maria,

so I don't want to hear you bitchin', okay?

- Yeah, but he shot the moon
on that hand, didn't he?
- Yeah, I saw that.

- So it helped you.
- Now... Okay, you're right.

You ain't walking outta here

with our grits, Worm.

You know the drill, okay? I'm not
gonna smoke 'em. I'll hold on to 'em.

if you want 'em back, you can
trade me for 'em, or try to play
double or nothing tomorrow.

Murphy! What the hell you sittin'
there for? You're processed. Come on.

Processed? This motherfucker's
gettin' the jump.

Come on, man, have some decency here, Worm.

You can buy all the smokes
you want in half an hour.

- What are you talking about?
I won these fair and square.
- You don't even smoke, Worm.

Jesus, you guys are such
fuckin' babies. You know that?

If you're determined to die
of cancer, you really oughta
learn how to play cards.

Ain't a good idea to add insult to injury, yo.

- That shit will come back and hurt you.
- You know what?

Not in this lifetime.
Enjoy your time.

Murphy.

Worm's dad
did the grounds, when he wasn't
too fuckin' drunk.

That's when we did 'em.

Of course, the grounds weren't all we did.

Worm put us into a scam a day
on all the young aristocrats
we went to school with...

selling 'em dime bags
of oregano, nunchakus
and firecrackers from Chinatown.

- Where's the rest?
- Kept us in lunch money.

- Thank you.
- Until the time we went for...

more than just pocket change and got caught.

We had the starting five take a dive
against Friends Academy.

The point guard snapped and gave Worm up.

They hauled him up before
the school board, offered him a deal.

Tell us who else was involved,
and we'll go easy on you.

Worm didn't say a fuckin' word.
Got himself expelled.

- I stayed in school and graduated.

- Crank the outside.

Not many guys would stand up
for a friend like that.

Ta-da!

- Mike McD. God. I knew you'd be here.
- Aw, man.

- You never let me down.
- I would have been there
every week if you let me, man.

I know, I know. I couldn't
let you see me in this shit hole.

- Look at you. You look great, man.
- You too, you too.

- Did they toughen you up in there?
- No, no.

It was a piece of cake.
Piece of cake.

Man, look at your ride. You've been
prospering while I've been away.

- What have you been up to?
- I borrowed it.

Whatever. Just get in it and
drive me far away from here.

There's like two whole economies in
there... there's cash and there's trade.

So I gotta keep three games
going at once, all right?

A game with the white guys,
a game with the brothers,
and a game with the guards.

And the trick is, I gotta take
enough cash off the white guys...

to lose it to the guards so that
they keep doing me favors and shit,

but I gotta trim enough smokes
off the black guys that I can
trade and keep myself...

in the style that I've grown
accustomed to, and all of this
without getting my ass kicked.

So you're working with a partner?

No. Who the hell
am I gonna trust in there?

- It's just me all alone.
- What's this? Come here.

- You like that? Isn't that beautiful?
- What is that?

It's like an ace up my sleeve.
What else?

Wait till I show you some of my chops,
man. I've gotten pretty blinding.

- It's like, it's like, you know...
- All right.

It's gonna blow your mind, blow your mind.

You been working?
Is your game sharp?

No, man, I'm off it.

What, are you...
you gettin' cold cards?

No, man, I mean I quit.

- What, are you shitting me?
- No, man, I...

- I got cleaned out.
- Mike McD? You lost?

Yeah, man, I... It was a real
blood game over at KGB's place.

You sat down with the Mad Russian
and he emptied your pockets?

Yeah. I didn't want to tell you
while you were in there.

I didn't want to dispirit you like that.

Jesus, what were you thinking?
So, you're just a student now?

- What are you doing for money?
- I'm driving Knish's truck.

Oh, God, you're killin' me. Mike, Mike,
we gotta get you back on the game.

- The old partners here,
we're gonna run like...
- No, no, no, I'm off it.

I mean, I really am. Done.

You are, huh? All right. I know a game
perfect for the two of us.

It's a berry patch right outside
New York City... prime pickings.

- I'll drop you... I'll drop you off.
- Okay.

- I mean it. No, I'm really off it.
- I know, I know.

This is it, this is it.

So get this, here's the plan.
I know this girl Barbara.

She's fuckin' hot. I was this close
to bangin' her when they sent me away.

She works as a hostess for all these
fuckin' trust fund babies in here.

She got me into their little game.

She introduced me as her cousin
from out of town who loves to
gamble but wants to learn poker.

That sounds solid.
That's a nice hookup.

It's all the way nice. There's only
one problem. I got this feeling.

- What feeling is that, exactly?
- You know this feeling very well.

- You know, when you got
your table all set.
- Uh-huh.

- Knife, fork, sauce,
A-1, Luger's, but...
- Yeah.

- You just don't have the stake.
- Exactly. Glad you understand.

A nickel would start me very nicely.

Whoa, Jesus, what have you been livin' on?

I'm livin' a little light, I told you.

- Anyway, that's $220,
so that'll get you started.
- $220, I mean...

Hey, thanks, but I mean, that's, like, 11 bets.

I mean, I can't even get a table on this...

Good, so forget this game. I'll
straighten you out in the city tomorrow.

No way. I gotta get started.

I mean, I'm already behind here.

You just got out.
What's the big fuckin' hurry?

The hurry is, other than you,
my friend, there's about five guys,

like, eagerly awaiting my release.

- How much do you owe?
- Like, ten.

- Ten?
- I can't even figure it with the juice.

Hey, look, I can get
started on this easy
if it's you and me working together.

I heard you asking before, and I hear
you asking now, but I can't do that.

I just can't do that.
I've made promises.

Hey, you know what? What am I saying?
I totally understand, I do.

It's fine. I'll make a couple of moves
earlier than I would have normally...

- But thanks, I appreciate it.
- Premium hands.

- I'll catch you in the city tomorrow?
- Yeah.

Hey, Mike, man.
Fuckin' great to see ya.

You too.

In Confessions of
a Winning Poker Player, Jack King said,

"Few players recall big pots
they have won, strange as it seems,

"but every player can remember
with remarkable accuracy...

the outstanding tough beats
of his career."

Seems true to me.
'Cause walking in here,

I can hardly remember how I built my bankroll,

but I can't stop thinking of how I lost it.

Mike.

- Hi.
- Barbara. Worm said
you'd be running a little late.

Just follow me.

I probably won't even sit.
You know, just kinda keep him company.

No, no, that's not gonna work.

Here's the play...
you're my new boyfriend,
you're looking for a regular game.

Really? Well, I'm not
much of a card player.

Bullshit. Worm tells me that's
precisely what you are.

My cut is 25 per cent.

- I see.
- Good. Come on.

Gentlemen.

- This is my boyfriend Michael.
- Hello, Michael.

Be nice to him.

- Leave him enough money
to buy me breakfast.
- [Laughter]

- Good luck.
- Thanks, sweetie.

Here, why don't you pull up a chair.

- Okay, this one's Chicago.
- You know Chicago?

- Uh, remind me.
- Stud game.

High spade in the hole wins half the pot.

Okay, well, deal me in, I guess.

- That's you.
- Oh, thanks.

Okay.

- That's two on you, Murph.
- Oh, yeah. Sorry.

- I'm in.
- I'm gonna make it five.

Hey, big spender.

Worm and I fall into our old rhythm
like Clyde Frazier and Pearl Monroe.

We bring out all the old school tricks,
stuff that would
never play in the city...

signalling, chip placing, trapping.

- We even run the old best hand play.
- Raise.

I can probably crack the game
just as quickly straight up,

but there's no risk in this room.

Now, some people might look down on
Worm's mechanics, call it immoral.

But as Canada Bill Jones said, "It's
immoral to let a sucker keep his money."

Like they teach you
in One-L...

caveat emptor, pal.

- I got the boat, queens over.
- [Chuckles]

He asked you if that stung, Birch.

Worm really has become an artist, too.

Discard culls, pickup culls,
overhand run ups, the Double Duke...

His technique is flawless.
But his judgment is a little off.

A few times, I have to fold the case
on him, just so it won't be obvious.

Still, he plays the part
of the loser to perfection.

Flush.

I got the full house.
I got the queens over the aces.

Ahh, fuck!
You know what?

- Fuck you and your never-ending
string of boats, okay?
- Hey.

Well, my Uncle Les says when the
money's gone, it's time to move on,

so enjoy it, you secret handshaking assholes.

Murph! Hey, come back any time.
Your money's always good here.

Good night, Mike. See you next time.

You guys, uh, wanna keep playing?

How'd we do?
Oh, beautiful.

Fuckin' assholes, they deserved it.

All right, $300, that's your cut.

- Thank you very much, boys.
- Hey, you were great. Great.

- When can we do this again?
- No, no, it was a one-time thing for me.

- Just because.
- Forget it.

- Uh, two weeks.
- Two weeks? Okay. Okay.

Hey, thanks a lot. Yeah.

Hey, I had to try, right?

Bye.

Hey, how'd you know I was coming back?

That's easy.
Who's your favorite actor?

Clint Eastwood. The Outlaw Josey Wales,
man. The Man with No Name.

He always doubles back for a friend.

Hey, we made good time.
Wanna get breakfast?

No, I gotta get home. If she
hasn't already changed the locks on me.

Just do me a favor.
Give me five minutes.

Get me straightened out.

This may not look like Teddy's place,
but it ain't the Ivy Leagues either.

So don't fuck around.
You gotta play on your belly.

All right.
No problem.

Hey, you know I have no problem
with the way you help yourself,

but these guys are fast company.

- They'll spot every move.
- Tough customers, huh?

- Yeah. I'm serious.
- All right.

- You won't just get
a finger up your spine.
- Okay, I hear ya.

I'm playing straight.

Michael McDermott.

- How you doin', Mikey?
- Good, how you doin'?

Good. You know, um,

the computer tried to delete you last week.

- Oh, yeah?
- But I knew you'd be back.

Oh, no, I'm not back, I just...

- It's good to see you.
- Good to see you, too.

Um, this is Les Murphy.
He's like my brother.

Call me Worm.

Hey. Don't wiggle away.

Hey, what's she wearing the button for?

They're wired right into the precinct.
They got 'em on the payroll.

- What are they playing?
- Uh, 20-40 forced rotation.

It's the only game going right now.

Is that Fat Greggie sitting 20-40?
The game's that soft?

Yeah. It's a real live game.
So, you guys gonna play?

- No.
- Hell, yeah, I'm gonna play.

- Oh, come on, you're not
gonna walk away from this.
- Not gonna happen.

Mike, we could cut this room up in an hour.

All right, run along, then.
Say hi to her for me.

- Me, too.
- I will. Take care of him.

Jesus. What a fuckin' waste.

Do you believe that?
She's really got him by the balls.

- That's not so bad, is it?
- Depends on the grip.

- Come on, give me $2,000.
- On the finger?

You heard Mike.
He's good for it. Come on.

Look, I'm gonna triple that
in half an hour, princess. Let's go.

Okay.

Hey.

Reunion run a little late?

I was gonna call,
but I didn't want to wake you up.

It's okay.
I wasn't sleeping.

Well, why don't you change and we'll get a cab.

Um, why don't you just go ahead,
and I'm gonna jump in the shower.

And if I miss a little bit
of the Mulligan meeting,
just cover for me, all right?

Hey.

At least give me a story.
You know, I mean...

I mean, tell me you were
out drinking till you threw up.

Tell me you were getting
lap dances over at Scores.

- I don't care, just give me something.
- I was entertaining Worm.

- Uh-huh.
- The least I can do for the guy.

- So, you were nowhere near a card game.
- Sweetie.

What?
I'm asking you a question.

- I'm just...
- No. I was nowhere near a card game.

All right?

All right.
I'll wait for you.

I mean, the key is a seamless
passing of the baton among the team.

I think the most important thing
is to be respectful to
the judges but not obsequious.

Now, wait a minute.
Make sure to be deferential.

Gene Marinacci won't buy deferential.

Oh, it's Gene, is it?

Well, I knew there was a reason
why you were lead counsel,

and it's got nothing to do
with your punctuality.

Sorry.
I couldn't find a cab.

Anyway, when you make
the opening remarks, make sure
you stick to the fact pattern.

And use the right cites.
Use book cites, not Lexis.

Hi, Jo.

- Long time.
- Knish. How are you?

The same.

I don't mean to interrupt
you future magistrates and noblemen,

but l, uh, I need a word.

- Um...
- It's important.

Okay. Excuse me.

Sorry.

- I'll act as lead counsel.
- It's all right, Kelly.

We were gonna take a break anyway.

Coffee time.

The guy's a cheat.
He always has been.

Right now, he's over at Chesterfield's,
ruining your reputation...

with every lousy second he deals.

Shit. I told him.
Did anybody else see him?

Nobody saw... I heard it.
Snapping sound gave it away.

I didn't know him, I might not have noticed.

I turn around, and I see him
with the mechanic's grip, I know.

- You want one?
- Did you give him the office?

I tried to warn him, but
he looked right through me.

- All right, I'll go get him.
- No, no, no. He's okay now.

Most of those Georges are at the tail
end of a 36-hour session.

They can't see straight.
Come on, I'll buy you a cup of coffee.

But if he's still there
when Roman and Maurice start their game,

he's gonna wish he was still inside.

I'm gonna go get him.

Amarillo Slim, the greatest
proposition gambler of all time,

held to his father's maxim...

"You can shear a sheep many times,
but skin him only once."

Gotta bet my jacks.

This is a lesson Worm's never bothered to learn.

Hey, guys.

English only at the table, no Russian.

- What are you talking about?
- What am I talking about?

If you want to see
this seventh card, you're gonna
stop speaking fuckin' Sputnik.

- Oh, da, motherfucker.
- You're worried we might work together.

I'm sure you're just talking about perogies...

and snow and shit, but let's
cut it out, all right?

There's the river, down and dirty.

I think you got that ace,
Roman, but I'm gonna pay for it.

Okay, well,
I got the jacks. Come on.

- Ace.
- Oh, you got it.
- And six.

Wow, two pair.
But I got sevens, too, though.

- With my jacks.
- Motherfucker, slow rolling me
like that.

You said just jacks.

But you made me for the sevens,
Maurice. You're a player.

- Fuck!
- Hey, come on! Don't be a fuckin' baby.

- Hey, Maurice.
- Hey.

Hey, Mike, you here to play?
Come on, we need some new blood.

They're putting a fucking bracelet
on me tomorrow for four months.

- I already stuck two racks.
- Well, have a good rest, man.

Can I talk to you for a second, Cosmonaut?

No, man, I'm on a roll.
This is a very emotional game.

Gotta do it.

I counted these.

Leave it.
It's fine.

- What's going on?
- Where are you at?

I was pumped up eight G's. I was ready
to go on a run when you came along.

- All right, listen.
- Hey, wait, I want a hot dog.

You're in town for five fuckin' minutes,
you already got a sign on your back.

Oh, what, that fuckin' Knish rat me out?

You gotta stop listening to that guy, man.

He sees all the angles, but
he doesn't have the balls to play one.

Hey, that guy hasn't had to
work in 15 years, Worm.

You don't think that's work, what he does?

Grinding it out on his fuckin'
leather ass? No, thank you.

I thought so, too, all right?
Now I know what real work is.

Speaking of which, are you even gonna get a job?

Or are you just gonna go back
to printing those credit cards?

- Huh? You gonna go away again?
- I wasn't printing.

I was distributing. Distributing.
It's different, okay?

Second of all, I'm never going back there.

Stop worrying so much, okay?

Come here.

I just want you to think
long term, all right? Be smart.

Every place in Manhattan,
they all keep books, all right?

If you get listed as a mechanic,
then not only are you gonna
get the shit kicked out of you,

you're not gonna get a fuckin' game
anywhere in New York.

It's stupid.
It's just bad business.

Look, this is what I love about you...
you think about the big picture.

That's great, okay?
But it's not me.

I don't play the game straight up,
and then if I lose,

go get some real work or something, okay?

I see a mark, I take him down.

That's what I do.
That's the way I live.

I know. Listen, you're the guy
who taught me all the angles.

- But I'm not the guy
with my nose open right now.
- Aw, come on.

I'm not gonna preach to you, but those
two guys in there, they're not rabbits.

Roman and Maurice?
They're Russian outfit guys.

Not as bad as KGB, but you don't want
to be fuckin' with those guys.

With those fake
Versace shirts and shit? Jesus.

Look, you still got time.
Just go back in there, right?

Lose their fuckin' money back to 'em, all right?

Just make it look good.
Just catch a run of real shitty cards.

- Give it back to 'em.
- I can't. I can't.

I gotta put some scratch together, man.
I gotta get somethin' going.

Then go out to suburbia, man. Play
in a fuckin' dentist's game, okay?

- Go to Swan Meadow,
play in the golf pro game.
- That's an idea.

I'll definitely do that,
but I can't dump to these guys.

You got to.

All right, whatever, whatever.

Meet me at Stromboli's
in half an hour, all right?

I can't, I gotta go.
I have a meeting.

And then I gotta go to fuckin' Queens.
I gotta load the truck.

Jesus, man, you're such
a fuckin' workin' man now.
I'm never gonna see you.

- Make it look good.
I mean it, make it look good.
- You know me.

- So, how'd you do?
- Ah, so-so.

Six thousand, two thousand.

Oh, hold on.
Two more.

All right, so it's ten grand total,

take back the two we lent you,

give you the white meat.

You know what?

Why don't you give me all of it?

Usually, credit players
only leave with their profit.

Otherwise, the juice starts
five points a week on Mike.

Oh, okay.
We'll owe you.

Hey. I've been looking
all over for you.

Didn't want to be found.

You know, Petrovsky waited and waited.
So did the rest of the group.

- Jo, look, I missed one meeting.
- It's not about the meeting.

I don't care about the meeting. Do
you even know why I left this morning?

- I found that gangster's roll
in your pocket.
- It's not what you think.

- It's not what you think.
- Who do you think I am?
You lie right to my face?

Look, old days at least you never lied.

You lost everything,

but at least you never lied.

Jo, this wasn't even a real game.
This was like Wiffle Ball.

- Can you lose your rent
playing Wiffle Ball?
- No, I couldn't lose.

- That's the point.
- No, Mike, you can lose.

I watched you, I stood by you while
you lost everything before.

- I don't think I can go
through that with you again.
- Jo, I wasn't gonna lose!

Why does this still seem like gambling to you?

Why do you think the same five guys
make it to the final table...

at the World Series of Poker every single year?

What are they, the luckiest guys in Las Vegas?

- It's a skill game, Jo.
- Great. So why'd you
have to lie to me?

- Because I knew you wouldn't understand.
- Understand what?

Last night, I sat down at this card table.

I felt alive for the first time since
I got busted at KGB's joint, okay?

You just told me you felt alive for
the first time at a fucking card table.

- No, what...
- What's that supposed to
make me understand?

Midnight, gettin' uptight Where are you

- You said you need me
but it's quarter to 2:00
- I heard you was out.

Hey, fuckin' Grama.
How you doin'?

- I was just thinkin' about you.
You know, I could use you.
- Oh, yeah?

See me in, like, two weeks.
I'll put you back on the payroll.

Well, I got some bad news for ya, Worm.
I'm out on my own now.

- Really?
- Yeah.

Go figure.

There were a lot of angry people when
you went away. A lot of people were mad.

I know, Grama, that's why I'm trying
to put together a roll here.

A lot of people coming up to me,
asking if I could help,

asking if I knew where to find you.

- So, it got me to thinkin'.
- Really, you thinkin' now? That's big.

Hey, Jesus! Come on!
Take it easy.

It's just a friend of mine.

Hey! Easy, easy, easy, easy.
God!

Get the fuck outta here.
What did I say?

- Hey, man, take it easy!
- Get the fuck outta here!

Okay.
Here's what I'm thinkin'.

Instead of you owing 15 grand spread out
to five guys, you owe 25 to me.

What? Where the fuck
do you get off? 25 grand?

Where the fuck do I get off?

Ohh.

Here's how it is. 25 grand,
and the juice is still runnin'.

Jesus Christ.

What the fuck are you doin', man?
You were my partner.

No, no, I was your lackey.

But I learned a few things, Worm.

I consolidated your outstanding debt.

Where'd you get the scratch for that?

You've been rolling fags in the Village again.

Still a wise ass. Unbelievable.

What I did was go partners
with an old friend of yours.

Teddy KGB backed me.

Bullshit.
Bullshit.

Teddy's got plenty of goons.

Why would he put you under his flag?

Because as soon as he heard your name,
he became real excited for the prospect.

What, so you bought me up, Grama?

Yeah, got a real sweet deal, too.
30 cents on the dollar.

There's not a lot of faith in you
out there in the business community.

Great, so you're a banker now, Grama.
That's really classy.

Not exactly. I don't have to tell you
my collection methods.

Oh, God. All right, look.

Just take it easy, all right?

I'll scrape something together,
and I'll find you this week.

- That's just what I figured.
- No, no, no.

- So I'm gonna take what you
got on you right now.
- Here. Fine.

Have yourself a ball, okay?

God!

Damn!

Excuse me.

Mind if I sit?

Michael.

Please, please.
Sit, sit.

That was a nifty trick the other night.

- It was wonderful.
- Thank you.

Marinacci and the D.A. were ready to cut
cards for your services at that point.

Of course,
it was an altogether different trick,

that disappearing act...

you pulled today at your group's meeting.

- Yeah. Well, I figure
I owe you an explanation.
- Ah, not to me.

I'm sure there's a good reason you left.

You'll just have to
work harder. Prepare.

And smooth things out with the others.

Right. Yeah.
Okay.

- Okay, well, thanks.
- Stay. Take a drink.

- Jamie?
- Yeah?

- Another glass, darling.
- Sure.

- What are you drinking?
- Gin. Always gin.

- Here you go.
- Thanks, dear.

Thank you.

I know a magician doesn't
divulge his secrets, but...

I'm no magician.

Well, if it wasn't magic,

how did you know what everyone held?

It's a combination of things.

Um, I was watching when the cards came out.

That's... That's just an old habit
with me, like breathing.

You watch the cards.

I watch the cards also, but I watch
the players reacting to the cards.

That's how I knew the D.A.
made his two pair,

and Judge Kaplan missed the flush.

I was watching their eyes
when they checked their river cards.

- Their faces tell you everything.
- You watch the man.

I... I never knew you had
to calculate so much at cards.

All right, here's the thing.
You only play premium hands.

You only start with jacks or better split,

nines or better wired,
three high cards to a flush.

If it's good enough to call, you gotta
be in there raising, all right?

I mean, tight, but aggressive.
And I do mean aggressive.
That's your style, Professor.

I mean, you gotta...
you gotta think of it as a war.

You are officially never
invited to our game again.

I don't blame you. Put a guy
like me in a game like that,
the cards don't even matter.

I'll play it blind.

Michael,

- May I tell you a story?
- Please.

For generations,
men of my family have been rabbis.

In Israel, before that in Europe.

It was to be my calling.
I was quite a prodigy.

The pride of my yeshiva.

The elders said I had
a 40-year-old's understanding...

of the midrash by the time I was 12.

But by the time I was 13,

I knew I could never be a rabbi.

Why not?

Because for all I understood of the Talmud,

I never saw God there.

- You couldn't lie to yourself.
- I tried.

Tried like crazy.

I mean, people were counting on me.

But yours is a respectable profession.

Not to my family.

My parents were destroyed,
devastated by my decision.

My father sent me away to New York...

to live with distant cousins.

Eventually, I...
I found my place,

my life's work.

What then?

I immersed myself fully, I studied the minutiae,

I learned everything I could about the law.

I mean, I felt deeply inside
that it was what I was born to do.

- And did your parents get over it?

- No.

I always hoped that I would find...

some way to change their minds, but...

They were inconsolable.

My father never spoke to me again.

If you had to do it all over again,

would you make the same choices?

What choice?

The last thing I took away
from the yeshiva is this...

We can't run from who we are.

Our destiny chooses us.

Hey.
L'chayim.

Hey.

Hey, where you been?
I've been freezing my ass off.

- What happened?
- Ah, ran into a door.
Don't worry about it.

- What happened?
- Hey! She crossed her legs
too fast, all right?

- Just mind your own business.

- You comin' up?

No, I've been standing out here
all this time just to say hi.

Listen, things haven't
been that smooth on the home front,

so tone it down a little, all right?

- Tone down what, motherfucker?
- Great.

Never mind.

When you become a big shot lawyer,
could you find us an elevator building?

Shut up.

What, did you get robbed?

Um, not exactly.

Wait, wait, wait.
Did she split on you?

Oh, God.

Oh, my God. Mike, she made off
with your sheets.

I always told her she'd be a good card player.

- Know exactly when
to release a shitty hand.
- Come on, Mike, forget that.

This girl is obviously
wrapped way too tight for living.

No, she was a good... I knew it.
I fuckin' knew it.

It's depressing.

You can't trust 'em.
You can't trust 'em at all.

I mean, look at you.
You domesticated yourself for this girl.

You took yourself out of the life.
You walked the fuckin' line for her.

And the minute you want a little
of it back, she walks out on you.

It's just like the saying says, you know?

In the poker game of life, women are the rake.

- They are the fuckin' rake.
- What the fuck are you talking about?

What saying?

I don't know.
But there oughta be one.

- You know what cheers me up
when I'm feelin' shitty?
- What?

Rolled up aces over kings.

- That right?
- Yeah.

Check raising stupid tourists

and taking huge pots off 'em.

- Yeah?
- Stacks and towers of checks
I can't even see over.

Playin' all night,
high-limit Hold' Em at the Taj.

- Where the sand turns to gold.
- Fuck it, let's go.

- Don't tease me.
- Let's play some fuckin' cards.

The poker room at the Mirage in Vegas...

is the center of the poker universe.

Doyle Brunson, Johnny Chan, Phil Helmuth...

The legends consider it their office.

Every couple of days
a new millionaire shows up...

wanting to beat a world champion.

Usually they go home with nothing but a story.

Down here, the millionaires are scarce
or they're playing craps,

but there's still
plenty of money for the taking.

In fact, on the weekends
you can't get a game in the city,

because all the New York rounders

are taking care of the tourists here.

Hey, hey, why don't you warm up
a seat for me. I'll catch up with you.

- What?
- Look.

- I got certain needs
I gotta attend to, okay?
- Hey, good.

- I mean, I'm overdue.
- Good, man, hey, I was startin'
to wonder about you.

I thought, maybe, you know,
the boys upstate brought about
a few changes in you.

Hey, in your dreams, lover.

- Hey, Mikey!
- Hey.
- Hey, Mike.

This is beautiful.
Welcome to the Chesterfield south.

- Ho!
- Changing $500.

Come all the way to Atlantic City
just to see your mugs, huh?

Twice in one week.

For someone who don't play, you spend
a lot of time in card rooms.

This is what I like to see, huh?

Mike McDermott where he belongs...
sittin' with the scumbags.

Tellin' jokes, draggin' the occasional pot.

Occasional? Yeah, like my ex-wife
occasionally went out with other men.

Forget her, Face. I was actually gonna
try and make some real money tonight.

But in honor of Mike's
alley-like return to the ring,

I'll sit with you all for a while.

Hey, don't do us any favors, Knish.

- They're about to go to
the board to fill these seats.
- Bet it.

I raise. You know, if we wanted
to take each other's rolls,

we could have just stayed home.

These two have no idea...

what they're about to walk into.

Down here to have a good time, they figure...

why not give poker a try?

After all, how different
can it be from the home games...

they've played their whole lives?

All the luck in the world isn't
gonna change things for these guys.

They're simply overmatched.

We're not playing together,
but then again, we're not playing
against each other either.

It's like the Nature Channel. You don't
see piranhas eating each other, do you?

They wear their tells
like signs around their necks.

Facial tics, nervous fingers.

A hand over a mouth.

The way a cigarette is smoked.

Little unconscious gestures
that reveal the cards in their hands.

We catch everything.

If a fish acts strong, he's bluffing.

If he acts meek,
he's got a hand. It's that simple.

- How are you, you workaholics?
- Worm.

Good to see ya.
Glad you're out.

Number's changed, of course.

Lotta games this weekend,
so you're gonna need the number.

- I'll give you a ring.
- Hey, Worm?

Do they allow people like you
in places like this?

Zagosh, when you get yourself a job,
then you can be my fuckin' P.O.

How about that?

Now, let's get started, shall we?

I'm sorry, sir.

You can't take chips
from another player at the table.

We all know each other here.

We're like friends, so if nobody
complains, do you have a problem?

- It's all right.
- No problem.

Sir, you have to buy 'em from me.

Fuck this low-limit shit.
Can we go get something to eat?
I got comped at the noodle bar.

I want to talk to you.

Look who's treatin' to a free meal.

Don't let that M.S.G. fuck
up your head more than it is, Mikey.

You keep grinding out that rent money,
Joe. It's noble work you're doing.

So, hey, uh, Nick the Greek.

What's with kitin' my checks?

- I'm on empty, that's why.
- You are? You're tapped again?

I mean...
How much was the hooker?

Mike, please. Relaxation therapist.

Okay?

- It's not where it went.
- Wait a minute.

It went to Roman and Maurice?

I told you, man, you didn't have to
give it all back to 'em.

Take a little money for your time, you know?

Hey, that's not where it went either.

- I ran into Grama tonight.
- Yeah?

Yeah. He took
everything I had.

You're kiddin' me.
Wait, who's he working for?

Well, he's sorta out on his own.

This fucker went around
and bought up all my debt. Grama.

That turncoat motherfucker.
Are you kiddin' me?

So what do you owe him?

I don't know. By his crazy fuckin'
gorilla math?

Like, 15.

- Fifteen? Fifteen?
- Yeah, I mean...

He says the juice has been running
the entire time on my ten.

- So, it's just like...
- Why didn't you tell me that, man?

Why did you not tell me that?
I could have paid that off.

- I had the... I had the money.
- Hey!

I'm not gonna sit in the can and have
my friend paying down my debt.

I'm not a leech, all right?

We can help each other, like always.
That's why we're here.

That's... That's why we gotta

get in the bigger game.

- Do you hear what I'm saying?
- All right. All right.

- Listen, man, I'll help you.
You know I'll help you, man.
- Yeah?

- I mean, fuck that guy.
We'll figure something out.
- Yeah.

How long should we wait?

I suggest we wait another five minutes,
and then choose another lead counsel.

Here he comes.

Mr. McDermott,
perhaps we can begin now.

I'm so sorry I'm late.

Come to order in the matter
of Slater v. New York State
Higher Education Services.

The facts have been stipulated,
the briefs have been read.

Lead counsel for plaintiff,
Mr. McDermott,

please proceed with oral arguments now.

If that is convenient for you.

Yes, it is, and again,

I'm sorry, ah, that I'm late.

Um...

Well, I think clearly the, uh...

the case which controls the issue at bar
would be, uh, Texas v. Johnson,

- Which holds...
- Texas v. Johnson?

Mr. McDermott, that is a Supreme Court
free speech case...

that has no bearing in the premises.

Each group was apprised to ignore
that aspect of this matter...

and focus instead on the idea
of de facto segregation.

Right. Um, well...

Mr. McDermott has
been unreachable,

so I'll take over, if it pleases the court.

Someone saying something meaningful
would please us a great deal.

What we have here is a clear case
of gerrymandering,

impacting schoolchildren
and schools in the district...

that was created solely

to separate students by race.

Although not dispositive, the student
body is more than 99 percent white.

Well, that was impressive.

Usually you have to know something about
a case to give an opening statement.

Guys, what...
what can I say?

Hey, it worked out great
for me, McDermott. I think
I actually impressed Marinacci.

Jo.

- Jo. Jo.
- What?

We're not gonna talk?
You left me pretty quick there.

- You make it sound
as if it was my decision.
- Well, it wasn't mine.

I came home and you were gone.
You were just gonna drop me like that?

I learned it from you, Mike.

You always told me that this was the rule.

Rule number one: Throw in your cards
the moment you know they can't win.

- Fold the hand.

- Look, this is our thing
that we're talking about.

It's not some losing hand of poker.

I know exactly what we're talking about, Mike.

So, that's the last of it, then?

Yeah.

I mean, I'd say good luck, but I know
it's not about luck in your game.

Eric Seidel cannot win this hand,

and yet he doesn't know it.

Chan is trying to sucker him in
by taking his time.

Oh, look at that look of the defending champ.

And now Fifth Street,
a six of diamonds. No help.

Johnny Chan has a queen high straight.

Will Eric Seidel fall for the bait?

Yes, he's going all in, and Chan has him.

Johnny Chan, the master...

Yes, he's going all in, and Chan has him.

- Hello.
- Oh, hey, Mike. It's Petra.
Can I come up?

Yeah, I'll buzz you in.

Well, that's the important thing
with the game of Hold 'Em.

You're never down and out
until your chips are all gone.

- Hey.
- Hey.

- How you doing?
- Good.

I haven't seen the place in a while.

Looks about the same.

- You want some scotch or something?
- No, I'm fine.

- Oh, '88 World Series, huh?
- Yeah.

Johnny Chan.

Flops the nut straight and
has the discipline to wait him out.

He knows Seidel's gonna bluff at it.

- And yet he doesn't know it.
- Johnny fucking Chan.

Chan is trying to sucker him in
by taking his time.

Look at the control.
Look at that fuck.

He knows his man well enough
to check it all the way...

and risk winning nothing with those cards.

He owns him.

Will Eric Seidel fall for the bait?

Yes, he's going all in and Chan has him.

- Johnny Chan, the master.
- Poor Seidel.
Kid doesn't know what hit him.

Yeah, I know what that feels like.

It's like a locomotive
running through your stomach.

You feel gut-shot. Fuck it.
You didn't come here to talk about this.

What's going on?

- Tomorrow's a week.
- A week of what?

The first two thousand you owe the Chesterfield.

- Oh. Worm.
- Yes, it's kinda weird.

He'd just won eight grand.
Why go on the line behind another two?

So, he took, what, about eight
off of Roman and Maurice?

Yeah, yeah, he comes in after you leave,

sits for like another 20 more minutes,

cashes out for the full amount.

Maurice hasn't been back since. I think
he's been playing across the street.

But, uh, Worm's been around plenty.

He's run you up just under seven grand.

Well, do me a favor and just put him on his own.

- Yeah?
- Yeah, cut him off.

Um, I tell ya, I got a thousand.

I got a thou.
And that's, you know...

I just started coming back, so...

- Thanks for making it easy, Mike.
- Oh, yeah, yeah.

I'm, uh... I'm sorry to be back
over here for this reason.

- Don't worry about it.
- No, l... I like being here.

It's good to see you, Mike.

- I can stay.
- Listen, I tell ya, I'Il... I'Il, um...

I'll come... I'll come...
I'll see you down at the club.

- I'll come by this week.
- Yeah.

I know you're in here.

Mike?

Hey. I thought you
were the janitor, man.

It's a good thing Grama
doesn't know you as well as I do.

Come on. I'll play ya horse.
Fifty bucks a letter.

Yeah? When I win, are you gonna pay
me back with my own fucking money?

Oh, oh, easy. Relax. Don't wing it.
Just... Just step and throw.

You need to work on your accuracy.

Will you stop fucking around
for five goddamn minutes
for once in your fucking life!

Whoa, Jesus. What happened?
My old man just walked in the door.

I should fucking beat the shit
out of you the way he used to.

You remember when we found this place, man?

Yeah, I remember when we found this place.

You were hiding from Tommy Manzy

'cause you thought he was gonna
fucking pound you into oblivion.

Yeah, now, see?
What did I ever do to that guy?

You fucked his mother.

Yeah, but she was a good-Iooking
older woman. You gotta give me that.

You spent a year of your life hiding in
this fucking gym from that sick fuck...

until he pissed off
the wrong guy and someone dropped
a garbage can on his head.

What do you want me to say? Those
were wild times. You were there too.

Nothing's changed.
Nothing has changed.

You were hiding from your troubles then.
You're hiding from your troubles now.

I like to hide, and that's
part of the fun for me, you know?

I don't like running solo.

It's like I used to have a running
partner, you know what I'm saying?

If we fucked up back then and got caught,

the worst thing that was going to happen
was maybe catch a beating, get expelled.

But, man, you're fixing to go down hard,
and it almost seems like you want to.

Stop worrying so much about me, okay?
I'm turning things around.

I'm not gonna let anybody
drop a garbage can on my head.

No, no, you're gonna get out of the way.
It's gonna land on me.

I'll see ya.

Come on, Mike. Hey.
Come on, come on, come on.

I'm sorry, okay?
I'm sorry about the money.

I should've told you.

It's just... What do you want me to say?
It's fucking embarrassing.

l, like, just get out,
I'm in a big fucking hole.

I need something to get goin'.
I gotta get started.

And?

Well, I'm not gonna lie.
There's been some reversals.

- Some reversals.
How much money do you have?
- Nine hundred.

I mean, I caught a frozen wave of cards
like you fucking read about.

I think I'm getting you outta hock,
I find out I'm seven grand in.

I know, man. I was really...
I was really up big.

I was cruising along.

I tried to beat that blackjack game
at the Horseshoe Club in Brooklyn.

- That place is a mitt joint.
- I know. It was,
like, ouch. I'm so stupid.

I got so good with this,
I thought I could neutralize 'em.

You're really jamming me up
here, man. Seven grand.

- I know.
- That's it. I can't go any deeper
than that. You're off the tip.

- I understand. That's okay.
- And you gotta talk with Grama.

- You gotta square things
away with Grama.
- No way, Mike.

I'm not talking to that fucking Judas.

You think there's any other way?

I know all the reasons I shouldn't be here,

but sometimes reasons don't matter.

You see, no one's ever stood up for Worm.

The guy's been kicked around
his whole life, from his father on down.

Maybe he's not the same guy
he was when he went away,

but I can't give up on him that easy.

I'm all he's got.

Oh, what the hell.

- Hi, boys.
- Hi.

You cops?
You look like cops.

- We're not cops.
- You wanna twirl then?

No, no, we're just here to see Grama.

Jesus.

- You sure about this?
I got a bad feeling.
- That's all right. Just...

Just let me do the talking, all right?

Hey, Grama.

- Long time.
- Mike.

Hey, Worm. It's good you came.
That's real smart thinking.

So, did you bring him along
to help carry all my money?

Uh, there's no money today.

No money?
There's gotta be some money.

Come on. Get outta here.

He's not kidding.
I got nothing.

You owe 25. I'll take
the rest in five days.

- Five grand in a week,
and you keep the juice going...
- Shh. Quiet.

You gotta catch 'em in the act.

Get in your hole, you bitch!

- Christ.
- Fucking dog.

You can't let 'em get away with it
or else they think they run the place.

- So, where were we?
- Five grand.

In a week. Grama, we want what
you want. We wanna square this thing.

But three days... three days
is impossible. All right?

No one's saying you're not the man. Just
think of this as a business decision.

Look, he just got out.
Let's put him on a plan.

No, no, no, no, no.
This isn't The Money Store.

We're not negotiating here.
I tell you how it works.

Well, then, I'm asking.

So, you're looking for a
little grace, Lester, some charity?

You know what, Grama?
I need your fucking charity
like I need your cock in my ass.

- Shut the fuck up!
- It's too late for him to shut up.

- Hey, listen! He's good for it.
- He's good for it, Mike?

If you think he's good for it, it's on you too.

Then it's on me too.

- Fifteen large, five days,
or I start breaking things.
- I hear ya.

Get the fuck outta here.

Piece of shit.

Now, what the hell are you doing?

I'm not gonna get down on my knees
for that jerk-off.

All I said is just keep
your mouth shut for five seconds.

- Shit. I'm sorry.
- Goddamn it.

That's it.
I'm really sunk now.

No, 15 grand in five days.
I can do that. I've gone
on rushes like that before.

Ah, under optimum conditions
with a bankroll, maybe.

- But what have you got on you?
- Got, like, 350.

Ah, that's 1,200 between us.
We might as well play the fucking Lotto.

No, man, no. Listen. Find the games,
scout 'em out, I sit, I mop 'em up.

You know, we might have a shot at this...

if we sat together and just did our thing.

I'm not gonna do that.
I'm gonna do this straight up.

- Oh, fuck, man.

- I mean it.

- Well, where do you wanna start?
- There's a 30-60 at the Chesterfield.

Come on, listen... there's the 4:00 a.m.
in Woodside. There's the Greeks.

All right, there's a union game in Jersey.

- I know a guy
whose cousin can get us in.
- All right.

- There's four.
- There's a cigar shop in Brooklyn.

- It's like an easy clean.
- There's a golf pro game
in Riverdale. That's six.

- You sure you're up for this?
- I'm fucking up for this.

An 80.

I bet the full amount.

The full amount, huh?
Well, let me look at you here.

Nope. You didn't do it this time.
I'm gonna raise you.

- I don't know.
- The bet's 50.

I kinda like this robusto.

A nice, nutty finish.

I love the Cameroon wrapper
on this baby. Nice and oily.

I'll call.
What do you got?

I have what's known as the wheel.

It's got earthy tones, a smooth draw,
enough kick to win me the Hi and the Lo.

Call.

- Trip aces.
- L... I only got a pair.

- Jacks.
- What did you think he had?

Does he look like a man beaten by jacks?

Jacks are a monster compared
to the crap you play, Taki.

- Ah, fuck you. Fuck you.
- Fuck me? Fuck you!

It's only money. I bet.

Then let's get some in there.

- Make it five.
- You're raising me 300, kid?

I call your 300.

- How much is in there, Weitz?
- About 1,500. 1,500.

Here's a thousand. There's 500.

I bet you the pot limit, kiddo.

Are you sure on that, Goldie?

You might want to leave
a little something for
your daughter's riding lessons.

There's a lot more where that came from, Weitz.

Take it down.

I got shit.
I bluffed the big ringer.

Let's go. Let's go.

Get up. Get off your ass.
We're done. Come on.

Anytime, anyplace, anywhere...
Oh, by the way, anybody.

Buy some real jewelry,
you fucking cheap bastard.

Unbelievable.

- What were you doing in there?
- I didn't have it.

You didn't have it?

Since when you have to have it to
take a pot off a hump like that?

- A grade schooler would've
played back at that guy.

- I was waiting the guy out.

Eventually, he was going to bluff
at the wrong pot. I was gonna take him.

We don't have time.
That guy was papier-mache.
You gotta make strong moves.

The move was folding. I can't lose
what I don't put in the middle.

Oh, Jesus, you know what?
Fuck all that 'cause we needed that pot.

Well, what are we up to?

That's like seven.
Seven.

With that pot you just dumped
on that fucking V-neck sweater,

we would've had ten.

Look at you. One 64-hour session,
and you need a nap.

- No time for a fucking nap.
- No, we don't. That's all right.

Come on.
I know what you need.

I know... I got just the place
for you. Yeah, yeah.

Feel like I'm gonna get whacked
sitting here like this.

We got 7,300, Mike.
We gotta double that in two days.

Well, we're gonna get close. I'm sure
if we come up a little short, Grama...

We come up even a little short,

Grama will shoot us and bury us
in a hole somewhere.

Now, I know this game up in Binghamton.

- In Binghamton?
- Yeah, yeah.

It's like 16 or 17 guys.
Two full tables. All municipal workers.

They come play right after
they get their paychecks. It's very fat.

Are you sure? Binghamton's
five hours each way.

Well, look, I figure there's
15 or 20 grand in that room, okay?

If we get even half of that, we're home.

Lead me to it.

- Municipal workers, huh?
- What? These guys work for the city.

They work for the state, you idiot.

Oh, this is just stupid.

Look, we're here, okay?

- You got any better ideas?
- How the hell am I supposed
to even get in this game?

No, it's easy.
The whole time I was in the joint,
I was just dumping money to guards.

This one guy, Pete Frye, I probably lost
like ten grand over 18 months.

I mean, he thinks I'm a total fish.

He told me anytime I wanted a game
when I got out, just look up his nephew.

You just go in there,
you ask for Sean Frye, you're in.

You're gonna clean this game up.
These guys are total suckers.

All right. Give me,
like, eight hours.

- Come back at 7:00, 7:30.
- What am I gonna do for eight hours?

- Why don't I come in?
I'll sit for a little while.
- No.

- No, not a chance.
- I'll sit at the other table
and play straight.

You wanna play straight? You go
in there, I'll be back in eight hours.

Aw, Jesus.

All right, all right. I'll go find
a fucking bowling alley.

I don't know.

Excuse me.

- Can I help you?
- Yeah, I'm looking for Sean Frye.

Yeah, right over there in that cap.

Thanks.

Let's go.

- Sean Frye?
- That's right.

Yeah, your Uncle Pete told me
to come by if I ever was around here.

You one of his students?

Oh, no, no, no, no.
I... I wasn't inside.

- You know him from hunting then, huh?
- Yeah, yeah, actually.

I met him over at, uh... He took me
for like a grand over at the lodge.

Well, that's the buy-in here.
We play 20-40 Stud.

- Grab a seat.
- Great.

- How you doing? I'm Mike.
- How you doing? Vitter.

- Osborne.
- Hi.
- This is Whitley.

Bet 40.

Back at ya.

- All right.
- You and me, Mike.

Another 40.

All right, 40 it is.

- Flush.
- Mm.

Generally,
the rule is, the nicer the guy,
the poorer the card player.

And these guys, despite being cops,
are real sweethearts.

I'm right on schedule, up 4,200.

The morning can't get here soon enough.

Holy shit! That's a hell of an elk.

My grandfather got that one.
Ain't that a beauty?

- Hey, fellas.
- Hey, Bear!

Met this guy down at the bowling alley.
Says he likes to play cards.

Well, you've come to the right place.

This is Whitley. Osborne.
This guy's name is Mike.

- Mike? How are ya? Les Murphy.
- This is Vitter.

- So, what are you guys playing?
- 20-40 Stud.

Okay.
Deal me in.

All right, your money's good here.

Give him some chips, start playing some cards.

Everybody ante.

Let's play some cards.

- Ace high bets.
- Well, I like what I have.

The bet is 20.

I know that look.
I'm gonna fold.

Fold too.

I'll take it.

- Yeah, everybody ready? Fourth Street.
- Yes, sir.

Raise you.

- I'm in.
- Wow. Wow. A lot of action.

A lot of action.

- I got the flush.
- Show me. What you got in here?

- Jesus. Who wants more?
- I'm in.

- I'm in.
- Come on, come on.

I'm staging
a late-night comeback here.

Late-night rally.

Okay? Just to...
Just to warn you.

Ace high bets.

Uh, ace checks.

- Check.
- Check on an ace. All right. I'll check.

- Check.
- Check.

All right, free card.
Here we go.

- Hold on there a fucking second.
- Easy. What are you doing?

- Give me the deck.
- Relax, man. Don't get so agitated.

- Looks like we got a road gang here.
- A what?

- What are you... What?
- What the hell's going
on over here, Stu?

This son of a bitch is base dealing.

- Caught a hanger, Sarge.
- What? A hanger?

I don't even know what you're saying.

- He's saying you're dealing
off the bottom of the deck.
- Oh, God. Come on, guys.

- What did he give him?
- To me?

- Seven of hearts.
- You boys professionals? You working?

I was winning before this guy got here.

Okay, okay. Let's let the cards
do the talking.

If the seven didn't help you,
we'll listen to what you have to say.

Ozzy, turn the cards.

Come on! It's three of a kind!

- Shut up!
- I'm just sayin', it's three of a kind.

One last thing, Stu.

Scumbag!

Hey, all right, take it easy.

Aren't you supposed to read us our rights?

Here's your fuckin' rights!

Fuck you!

Get the fuck outta here,
you cocksuckers! Shit!

Aw, Jesus!

Worm.

Worm?

Hey, Les.

Hey.

Hey, you all right?

Mike?

Yeah.

You should've played those kings, Mike.

Aw, you're an asshole.

I know. I know.
I'm sorry.

They took every fucking nickel.

I think I got 300 in my boot somewhere.

Oh, look at you.
Fuck!

Fuck, I cannot believe I caught a hanger.

- Aw, it's never happened,
I swear to God.
- Where's the car?

- God, I think I cracked a rib.
- What the fuck were you thinking?

- I was trying to give us an edge.
- I had 'em.

Hey, I'm sorry we got banged up, all right?

I took a shot and I missed.
That happens.

- Fucking happens
all the time around you.
- What, it doesn't happen to you?

You're the guy who flushed his whole
fucking bankroll on one hand, Mike.

- Oh, hey, fuck you, man.
That was different.
- Why? Explain that to me.

Why different, huh?
What makes you so fucking special?

How come all your moves

are so smart and noble...

and I'm always the idiot piece of shit?

You act like you're the only one
with any fucking ambition.

What's your ambition, man? Tell me.
I don't know. What is it?

- I don't even know.
I don't think like that.
- No, you don't think.

No, I don't think like you!

You always think you can beat the game
straight up. That's not me.

- I told you, I'm always gonna
look for that edge. Always.
- What's the edge now?

We owe 15 grand in a day.
What do we do?

It's easy. We get
the fuck outta Dodge, all right?

We just steer clear of the city for a while.

We'll hit the road. We'll be up again
in no time. This'll all blow over.

- We'll have a ball.
- Not a fucking chance
I'm gonna live like that.

- You talk to Grama.
You get him to stake me.

- It's not gonna work, okay?

We're not dealing with Grama.

You said Grama's on his own.

- You told me Grama's on his own.
- KGB bankrolled him.

- So you've just fucked us
right in the ass.
- Yeah, all the way, okay?

So you see what I'm saying?
No fooling around. It's highway time.

Are you with me or not?

No, I'm not this time.

- Give me the keys.
- You're really gonna go back there?

Yeah.

I'll see you when I see you.

Hey. At least you're
rounding again, right?

You're gonna thank me for that someday.

Fold or hang tough.
Call or raise the bet.

These are decisions you make at the table.

Sometimes the odds are stacked so clear,
there's only one way to play it.

Other times, like holding a small pair
against two over cards,

it's six to five, or even money, either way.

Then it's all about feel, what's in your guts.

Well, look at you.

Look at me.

Come in.

No.

- Where's your friend?
- Uh, he's gone.

- He's gone.
- So you brought my money?

- I'm a little short.
- How short?

The whole way.

There must be some kind of story.

Well...

as you can see, I can't pay you.

I see you're banged up pretty good.

You never should've vouched for that scumbag.

Maybe not.

- You're leaving me no outs here.
- Why?

I can't trust you two aren't playing me.

I'm not the one working with a partner here.

You wanna take it up with KGB,
you go right ahead.

Otherwise, you got one day,
or this'll feel like a Swedish massage.

- Hey.
- Hey, what's up?

You look like Duane Bobick
after one round with Norton.

- What the fuck happened to you?
- Ah, Worm.

When are you gonna listen?

I'm listening.

What do you need?
500? A grand?

- Huh?
- I need... I need 15,000.

- Fifteen?
- Yep.

I need a blow job from Christy Turlington.

- Get the fuck outta here. $15,000?
- Seriously, Joey.

What can you do for me?
Five hundred dollars is not

even gonna get me started.

Goddamn it, Mike, if 500 won't
help, what's two grand gonna do?

What kind of trouble you in?

I'm in the worst kind, with the worst guy.

- KGB?
- Yep.

Come here.

Didn't I tell you...

to never let that guy get a hold of you?

- You told me a lot of things.
- Yeah, yeah. And you don't listen.

I tell you to play within your means,
you risk your whole bankroll.

I tell you not to
overextend yourself, to rebuild,

you go into hock for more.

I was giving you a living, Mike,

showing you the playbook
I put together off my own beats.

That wasn't enough for you...

This is one time I don't need
you to tell me how I fucked up.

I know I fucked up.

What I need from you is money.

- I need whatever money you can give me.
- See, that's the thing.

This time there is no money.

I give you two grand,
what's that buy you? A day?

No, I give it to you, I'm wasting it.

- That's fucking great.
- You did it to yourself.

You had to put it all on the line
for some Vegas pipe dream.

Yeah, I took a risk.
I took a risk.

You see all the angles.
You never have the stones to play one.

"Stones"?
You little punk.

I'm not playing for the thrill
of fucking victory here.

I owe rent, alimony, child support.
I play for money.

My kids eat.

I got stones enough
not to chase cards, action...

or fucking pipe dreams

of winning the World Series on ESPN.

You want me to, uh, call some people,

try and buy you some time, I will.

Place to stay, or the truck.
No problem.

But about the money,
I gotta do this. I gotta say no.

That's fine.
I understand.

- Hey, listen.
- What?

I put it all on the line.
That's true.

And you know what?
It wasn't a bad beat.

I wasn't unlucky.

I got outplayed.
I got outplayed that time.

But I know I'm good enough to sit at that table.

It's not... It's not
a fucking pipe dream.

I don't doubt your talent.

I never...
I never told anybody this.

About eight, nine months ago,

I'm at the Taj, it's late,

and I see Johnny Chan walk in.

And he goes,
he sits 300-600.

And the whole place stops
when Johnny Chan walks in.

Everybody puts an eye on him.

After a little while,
there wasn't a crap game going...

'cause all the high rollers
are over there watching him.

Some are playing with him, giving
away their money to this guy to say...

"Oh, I played
with the World Champion."

And you know what I did?
I sat down.

Nah, you need 50, 60 grand
to play right in that game.

Well, I had six, but I had to know.

What happened?

Played tight for an hour. I folded
mostly, and then I made a score.

- Wired aces or kings?
- Rags.

I had nothing.
But he raised.

And I just decided, you know,
I don't care about the money.

I'm just gonna outplay the guy.

I'm just gonna outplay this guy this hand.

- I re-raised.
- Re-raise.

- You played right back at him, huh?
- Oh, yeah.

And he just comes right back over the top of me,

trying to bully me like
I'm some fucking tourist.

I hesitate for two seconds.
I re-raised.

And he makes a move toward his checks,
and he looks at me.

And he looks at his cards,
and he looks at me again.

And he mucked it.
I took it down.

"Did you have it?"
"I'm sorry, John. I don't remember."

I got up, and I walked to the cashier.

I sat with the best in the world, and I won.

You put a fucking move on Chan,
you son of a bitch.

So that's why you made that run on KGB's place.

That's right.

And I'll do it again if I can.

Well, then I'm rooting for you, Mike.

I'll see you around, Knish.

This is temporary?
Will you be back next semester?

Oh, I think we both know I'm no lawyer.

I hope my story didn't discourage you.

No. It inspired me.
I think I was on my way out anyway.

- But now you're here.
- That's right.

- You're in trouble?
- Yes, sir, I am.

Uh, not with the law.
I owe.

- A gambling debt?
- Yeah.

It's not mine. It's, uh...
I vouched for the wrong guy.

Um, so now it's on me.

I understand.

So, what will it take
for you to be free of this?

- I need 15,000 tonight.
- Michael!

Michael!

- You know, I'm not
a wealthy man, Michael.
- I know.

And it kills me to ask you, but...

I don't have any other play here.

So, uh, if you can help me at all...

I hate to see you like this.

I want to help you, Michael.
But $15,000, I... I...

I know.

If it must be tonight,

then ten is the best I can do.

Would you do that?

When my mother let me leave the yeshiva,

it nearly broke her.

But she knew...
She knew the life I had to lead.

To do that for another is a mitzvah.

And for that, I owe.

So you take this money...

and you get yourself out of this trouble.

You hear me?

I know you can.

I... I promise that I'm gonna...
I'll pay you back.

Good luck.

I've often seen these people,
these squares, at the table.

Short-stacked and long odds against,
all their outs gone,

one last card in the deck that can help them.

I used to wonder how they could let
themselves get into such bad shape...

and how the hell they thought
they could turn it around.

Just walking in here makes me queasy.

The brick walls.
The fucking mopes at the tables.

The musty smell. I feel like Buckner
walking back into Shea.

But what choice do I have?

So, you have my money?

- I owe you that money tomorrow, right?
- Da.

So it's still mine.

For the next eight hours, it is yours.

But if you don't have it all by then,

then you are mine.

Well...

I got $10,000.
I'm looking for a game.

- You sure?
- You heard me.

So, we'll play. Heads up.

We both start with a couple of racks.

Blinds, uh, 25 and 50?

And we don't stop until one of us has it all.

Let's do it.

I'm gonna raise.

Thousand straight.

Very aggressive.

A new day.

And you won't be pushed around.

But... I re-raise.

Five thousand.

Doyle Brunson says,
"The key to No-Limit...

is to put a man to a decision
for all his chips."

Teddy's just done it.

He's representing aces,
the only hand better than my cowboys.

I can't call and give him a chance to catch.

I can only fold,
if I believe him. Or...

I re-raise. I'm all in.

Take it down.

In a heads-up match,

the size of your stack is almost as
important as the quality of your cards.

I chopped one of his legs out in the first hand.

- Now all I have to do is lean
on him until he falls over.
- Check.

Bet a thousand.

Call. I'll call.

Check.

What's that, 2,500 there?
I'm gonna tap your tap.

Jacks up.

Very good.

Good hand.

Catching that Jack on the turn.

- You got lucky there.
- Yep, it was luck.

So, that's it then, hmm?

Just like a young man coming in for a quickie.

I feel so unsatisfied.

I'm sorry.

You must feel proud and good.

Strong enough to beat the world.

- I feel fine.
- Me too. I feel okay.

'Course maybe we check
with one other guy, see how he feels.

Grama!

I thought I smelled him.

I'll take what's ours.

'Course you could let it ride, Mike.

Take your chances.
You could let this happen, Grama?

Sure, partner.

He still has till morning to make good.

Uh, you know what? I got my
five grand here. That's just fine by me.

- I'm going home.
- Fine.

It's a fucking joke anyway.

After all, I am paying you with your money.

- What did you say?
- Your money.

I am still up 20 grand...

from this last time I stick it in you.

They're trying to goad me, trying to own me.

But this isn't a gunfight.
It's not about pride or ego.
It's only about money.

I can leave now, even with Grama and KGB...

and halfway to paying Petrovsky back.

That's the safe play.

I told Worm you can't lose

what you don't put in the middle.

- Deal 'em.
- But you can't win much either.

Checks!

- Double the blinds?
- Yeah.

Table stakes.

Good. Feel free
to reload at any time.

You must be kicking yourself...

for not walking out when you could.

Bad judgment.

But...

don't you worry, son.

It will all be over soon.

Okay.

Check.

No check here.
I tap you.

I'm laying this down, Teddy.

Top two pair.

It's a monster hand,
and I'm gonna lay that down...

'cause you got two-four, and I'm
not gonna draw against a made hand.

Lays down a monster.

Should have paid me off on that.

Why the fuck did you lay that down?

Wow.
Not hungry?

Mr. Son of a Bitch.

Let's play some cards.

The rule is this:

You spot a man's tell,
you don't say a fucking word.

I finally spotted KGB's.

And usually I would've let him
go on chewing those Oreos
till he was dead broke.

But I don't have that kind of time.
I've only got till morning.

Not even Teddy KGB's immune
to getting a little rattled.

Enough is enough, Teddy.
Finish the fucking kid off.

Hanging around.
Hanging around.

Kid's got alligator blood.
Can't get rid of him.

No, I'm not going anywhere.
Double the blind.

Okay.

I call.

Check.

Two grand.

All right, I'll call the two grand.
I'll gamble.

Don't splash the pot.

You're on a draw, Mike?
Go away.

This one is not good for you.

And in my club, I will splash the pot
whenever the fuck I please.

Okay.

I'm gonna check, Teddy.

That's right.

Big daddy...

bets...

the pot.

That's 4,400.

All right, I'm gonna call you, or else
I won't respect myself tomorrow morning.

Respect is all you'll have left in the morning.

Last card coming.

Check.

It hurts, doesn't it?

You can't believe what fell.

All your dreams... dashed.

Hopes down the fucking drain.

Your fate, he is sitting right beside you.

That ace could not have helped you.

I bet it all.

You're right, Teddy.
The ace didn't help me.

I flopped a nut straight.

Motherfucker!

- Motherfucker! That is it!
- That's it?

What the fuck you talking about?

- Take him down, Teddy.
- Nyet! Nyet! No more!

No! Not tonight!

This son of bitch,
all night he check, check, check.

He trapped me!

Well, you feeling satisfied now, Teddy?

'Cause I can go on busting you up all night.

Nyet! Nyet!

He beat me.
Straight up.

Pay him.

Pay that man his money.

Turned my ten grand into just over 60.

Paid 15 to Grama, six went back
to the Chesterfield.

As for Worm, well, I figure we're even.

And after the ten going back to the professor,

I'm back where I started,
with three stacks of high society.

Hey.

- You look like hell.
- Ah, well, you should've
seen me yesterday.

- Are you okay?
- Yeah, I'm okay. You?

Now I am.

So, you're outta here, huh?

Yeah, I'm... I figure
there's nothing left for me here.

Listen, um, will you give this to Petrovsky?

I... didn't want to wake him up.
It's still a little early.

Can I count on you to do that?

You could always count on me, Mike.

Thanks.

Take care, Jo.

Hey. Call me.

If you need a lawyer.

I will.

And I will.

Kennedy Airport.

- So, where you headed?
- I'm going to Vegas.

- Vegas, huh?
- Yeah.

Good luck, man.

People insist on calling it luck.

Thanks.

First prize at the World Series
of Poker is a million bucks.

Does it have my name on it?
I don't know.

But I'm gonna find out.

Printed in the USA
CPSIA information can be obtained
at www.ICGtesting.com
LVHW071948131223
766287LV00081B/1889